Cosmopolitan Hotels

teNeues

Editor: Martin Nicholas Kunz
Editorial coordination: Ulrike Paul
Introduction: Christiane Reiter

Layout & Prepress: Thomas Hausberg

Translations: AdeTeam
English: Dr. Andrea Adelung
French: Eric Lingo
Spanish: Miguel Carazo

Published by teNeues Publishing Group

teNeues Publishing Company
16 West 22nd Street, New York, NY 10010, US
Tel.: 001-212-627-9090, Fax: 001-212-627-9511

teNeues Verlag GmbH + Co. KG
Book Division
Kaistraße 18
40221 Düsseldorf, Germany
Tel.: 0049-(0)211-994597-0, Fax: 0049-(0)211-994597-40

teNeues Publishing UK Ltd.
P.O. Box 402
West Byfleet
KT14 7ZF, Great Britain
Tel.: 0044-1932-403509, Fax: 0044-1932-403514

www.teneues.com

ISBN: 3-8238-4546-2

Bibliographic information published by
Die Deutsche Bibliothek. Die Deutsche Bibliothek lists
this publication in the Deutsche Nationalbibliografie;
detailed bibliographic data is available in the Internet
at http://dnb.ddb.de

INTRODUCTION

For years, he had been a guest at the same hotel chain. And no matter what city he visited, he was always met in the lobby by an arrangement of plants highlighted by halogen spotlights, and softly bubbling fountains. In the room, the light switch was always exactly five centimetres above the night table, easily accessible even when he was half asleep, and the bathroom smelled like a mixture of cleanser and vanilla. Every three months, he would receive a colorful newsletter in his mailbox at home, as well as a card on his birthday, and when he had collected enough points on his customer card, he was allowed to reserve the Junior Suite with the large front windows.

It was all so pleasant—and so boring. In a time when travelling has become very predictable, when one can drink the same coffee and watch the same films in any given city on the planet, hotels have the opportunity to offer a city an individual face; to shine with a unique charm, to possess that special something, to feel like home, even be a real home. As tacky and cliché as that might sound: it is exactly what we want—we don't go to a hotel to "just sleep there", we live there. Just as in our own homes, we need our own hotel room; one that allows us to forget that other guests stayed there before us and more will come after we leave—a room that has personality and a sphere of privacy. By the way: private owners have long since recognized this trend—architectural magazines and books on design are packed with their magnificently furnished city hotels, all of which, however, are also often magnificently booked, such that one only knows them from word of mouth.

However, more and more large enterprises are now offering guests luxurious establishments, ones which effortlessly maintain a balance between innovation and timelessness, in which mass-produced products are as scarce as experimentally trendy design that likens safe style with stuffiness. In such hotels, clean, simple, and soothing lines are the rule, the trilogy of furniture, fabrics and colors will continue to be harmonious a decade from now, and art is perfectly positioned. These buildings possess a simple beauty which has made or can make them modern classics, and bring discovery, experience and distinctiveness back to travelling. Because, with details such as magazines placed as if randomly, a subtlety-lit bar, or simply a breathtaking view over rooftops, these hotels can awaken interest and curiosity in the city in which they are located.

This book is a collection of addresses from all around the world, in metropolitan areas such as London, Paris, Rome, New York, São Paulo and Sydney. If you stay in one of these hotels for a few days (or simply read about them on the only following pages), you will remember details that you hardly thought possible, you will recommend the establishment to close friends as an insider tip, and, most of all, you will return. Welcome home.

Christiane Reiter

EINLEITUNG

Er war schon seit Jahren Gast derselben Hotelkette. Und in welche Stadt er auch kam, immer begrüsste ihn in der Lobby ein Arrangement aus halogenbeleuchteten Grünpflanzen und leise plätschernden Brunnen, im Zimmer war der Lichtschalter genau fünf Zentimeter über dem Nachttisch installiert und selbst im Halbschlaf bequem zu erreichen, und im Bad roch es nach einer Mischung aus Weichspüler und Vanille. Alle drei Monate bekam er einen bunten Newsletter nach Hause geschickt, zum Geburtstag lag ein Glückwunschschreiben in der Post, und wenn er auf seiner Kundenkarte genügend Punkte gesammelt hatte, konnte er beim nächsten Mal die Junior Suite mit der großen Fensterfront reservieren.

Es war so angenehm – und es war so langweilig. In einer Zeit, in der das Reisen sehr berechenbar geworden ist, in der man in fast jeder Stadt der Erde denselben Kaffee trinken und denselben Kinofilm ansehen kann, haben Hotels die Chance, einem Ort ein individuelles Gesicht zu geben. Mit Geschmack, Eleganz und Charme zu glänzen, das gewisse Etwas zu besitzen, das man nur fühlen und nicht sehen kann, typisch einheimisch, ja, eine richtige Heimat zu sein. So kitschig und klischeebeladen das auch klingen mag: Es ist genau das, was wir uns wünschen – wir sind eben nicht „nur zum Schlafen" in irgendeinem Hotel, wir leben dort. Wie ein eigenes Zuhause brauchen wir ein eigenes Hotelzimmer; eines, das uns vergessen lässt, dass vor uns schon Gäste da waren und auch nach uns welche kommen werden, eines mit Persönlichkeit und Privatsphäre. Apropos: Privatbesitzer haben diesen Trend längst erkannt, Architekturzeitschriften und Designbände sind voll von ihren zauberhaft ausgestatteten Stadthotels, die allerdings oft auch so zauberhaft ausgebucht sind, dass man sie nur vom Hörensagen kennt.

Doch jetzt ziehen immer mehr große Unternehmen nach und öffnen ihren Gästen luxuriöse Häuser, die den Balanceakt zwischen Innovation und Zeitlosigkeit mühelos halten, denen Fließbandprodukte genauso fremd sind wie experimentell-modische Gestaltung, wo „stilsicher" nicht gleichzeitig „steif" bedeutet. In solchen Hotels führen klare und schnörkellose Linien ein unaufdringliches Regiment, der Dreiklang aus Möbeln, Stoffen und Farben wird auch in einem Jahrzehnt noch harmonisch sein, und Kunst macht genau dort Sinn, wo sie auftaucht. Schlicht schön sind diese Gebäude, die zu modernen Klassikern geworden sind oder werden können und die das Reisen wieder zu einer Entdeckung, zu etwas Erlebbarem und Einzigartigem machen. Denn mit einem wie zufällig hingelegten Magazin, einer dezent beleuchteten Bar oder einfach einem atemberaubenden Blick über die Dächer wecken solche Hotels auch Lust und Neugier auf die Stadt, in der sie stehen.

Dieses Buch versammelt Adressen in aller Welt, in Metropolen wie London, Paris, Rom, New York, São Paulo und Sydney. Wer in einem dieser Hotels einige Tage verbringt (oder vorerst auch nur die nachfolgenden Seiten durchblättert), wird sich hinterher an Details erinnern, von denen er vorher kaum wusste, dass es sie gibt, er wird das Haus nur seinen besten Freunden und nur als Geheimtipp empfehlen – und er wird vor allem wiederkommen. Willkommen zu Hause.

Christiane Reiter

INTRODUCTION

Depuis des années déjà, il était l'hôte de la même chaîne d'hôtels. Et quelle que soit la ville où il arrivait, une composition de plantes vertes éclairées par halogène et des fontaines aux doux clapotis l'accueillait dans le hall. Dans la chambre, un interrupteur était installé juste cinq centimètres au-dessus de la table de nuit. Même demi-éveillé, il pouvait accéder facilement à l'interrupteur. Dans la salle de bain, il régnait un mélange subtil de assouplissant et de vanille... Tous les trois mois, il recevait une Newsletter multicolore. Le jour de son anniversaire, il trouvait une lettre de voeux dans son courrier, et lorsqu'il avait collecté suffisamment de points sur sa carte-client, il pouvait réserver la prochaine fois la Suite Junior avec la grande baie.

C'était si agréable – mais c'était en même temps à mourir d'ennui... A l'heure où le voyage est devenu très prévisible, où l'on peut boire dans chaque métropole du globe le même café et voir le même film, les hôtels ont cette particularité de conférer à chaque endroit leur caractère inoubliable. Se distinguer par le goût, l'élégance et le charme, posséder le petit plus, que l'on ne peut pas voir mais sentir, ô combien familier, en un mot être une propre patrie. Aussi banal et chargé de clichés que cela puisse paraître, c'est précisément cela que nous recherchons – nous ne sommes pas là « pour dormir seulement » dans un hôtel, nous y vivons ! Nous avons besoin d'une chambre d'hôtel bien à soi tout comme d'un propre chez soi ; une chambre qui nous fait oublier que des hôtes nous ont précédés et que d'autres nous succéderons, une chambre alliant personnalité et sphère privée. A propos : les propriétaires privés ont reconnu depuis longtemps cette tendance. Les revues d'architecture et les ouvrages de design regorgent de ces hôtels situés en ville magiquement aménagés, qui sont la plupart du temps réservés comme par enchantement, de telle sorte que l'on ne les connaît que par ouï-dire.

Toutefois, de plus en plus de grandes entreprises suivent cette tendance et ouvrent à leurs hôtes la porte de maisons luxurieuses préservant sans peine le délicat numéro de funambule entre l'innovation et l'intemporalité. Les produits à la chaîne leur sont résolument étrangers tout comme la conception expérimentale soumise aux fluctuations de la mode. Mais en aucun cas, « avoir un style sans faille » ne saurait signifier simultanément « rester figé ». Dans de tels hôtels, des lignes claires et dénuées de fioritures donnent à l'ensemble un air discret. Le triple accord de meubles, d'étoffes et de couleurs sera sans nul doute harmonique encore dans une décennie, et comme chacun le sait, l'art n'a de sens que précisément où il intervient... Ces bâtiments sont tout simplement bouleversants de beauté et de simplicité : ils sont devenus des chef-d'œuvre classiques modernes ou ils sont en passe de le devenir. Ils rendent à nouveau le voyage digne de découverte, d'être vécu et unique en son genre. Car avec un magazine posé comme fortuitement, un bar éclairé de manière décente ou tout simplement une vue imprenable sur les toits, ces hôtels suscitent aussi l'envie et la curiosité de découvrir la ville, dans laquelle ils se trouvent.

Ce livre rassemble des adresses de tout premier plan dans le monde entier, dans des métropoles telles que Londre, Paris, Rome, New York, São Paulo et Sydney. Quiconque passe quelques jours dans l'un de ces hôtels (ou feuillette préalablement les pages suivantes) se rappellera ensuite de tous les détails qu'il soupçonnait à peine auparavant pouvoir exister. Il ne recommandera cet hôtel particulier qu'à ses meilleurs amis et sa recommandation sera un secret savamment distillé. Une chose est sûre et certaine : il reviendra. Bienvenue à la maison !

Christiane Reiter

Introducción

Él ya era cliente de la misma cadena de hoteles desde hacía años y, independientemente de la ciudad que visitaba, en el vestíbulo siempre era recibido por una combinación de plantas verdes iluminadas con lámparas halógenas y fuentes chapoteando silenciosamente; el interruptor de la luz estaba instalado exactamente cinco centímetros sobre la mesita de noche de la habitación y era fácil y cómodamente accesible incluso a duermevela, y en el baño olía a una mezcla de suavizante y vainilla. Cada tres meses recibía en casa un boletín informativo multicolor, el día de su cumpleaños tenía una carta de felicitación en el buzón, y cuando había juntado suficientes puntos en su tarjeta de cliente podía reservar otra vez la junior suite con la ventana de fachada grande.

¡Era tan agradable y al mismo tiempo aburrido! En una época en la que viajar se ha vuelto bastante calculable, en la que puede beberse el mismo café en casi todas las ciudades del planeta y ver la misma película, los hoteles tienen la oportunidad de asignar un aspecto individual a cualquier lugar determinado, brillar con buen gusto, elegancia y encanto, poseer esa peculiaridad que sólo pueda sentirse pero no percibirse, tener un carácter típico del lugar y convertirse en un verdadero hogar. Tan cursi y estereotipado como pueda sonar: Se trata justamente de lo que deseamos, pues nosotros no vamos a ningún hotel "sólo a dormir", sino que vivimos en el mismo. Al igual que en nuestra propia casa, también necesitamos una propia habitación en el hotel; una habitación que nos permita olvidar que antes de nosotros ya se alojaron otros clientes en la misma y que también se alojarán otros después de nosotros, y que tenga personalidad y esfera privada. A propósito: Los dueños de propiedades privadas han detectado esta tendencia hace tiempo; las revistas de arquitectura y los manuales de diseño están repletos de hoteles de ciudad de su pertenencia equipados de forma encantadora, pero que, sin embargo, con frecuencia se hallan tan encantadoramente completos que sólo se conocen de oídas.

Pero ahora existen cada vez más empresas importantes que contrarrestan la situación y abren a sus clientes las puertas de alojamientos lujosos que pueden mantener fácilmente el equilibrio entre innovación y atemporalidad, a los que los productos de las cadenas de montaje les resultan tan extraños como la creación de moda experimental, donde "estilo depurado" no es sinónimo de "rígido". En ese tipo de hoteles, las líneas claras y sin volutas lideran un regimiento discreto, el acorde perfecto entre muebles, tejidos y colores continuará siendo armónico transcurrida una década, y el arte tendrá sentido justo allí donde emerja. Estos edificios son hermosos sin más, se han convertido o podrán convertirse en clásicos modernos y podrán conferir nuevamente a los viajes un carácter de descubrimiento, de algo experimentable y singular, pues con una revista casualmente depositada, un bar iluminado con decoro o simplemente una vista impresionante por encima de los tejados, esos hoteles también despiertan el deseo y la curiosidad de la ciudad donde se encuentran.

Este libro reúne direcciones de todo el mundo, en metrópolis como London, Paris, Roma, Nueva York, São Paulo e Sydney . Quien se aloje unos días en alguno de estos hoteles (o sólo hojee en primer término las páginas que siguen a continuación) recordará posteriormente detalles que apenas sabía que existieran con anterioridad, sólo recomendará el hotel a sus mejores amigos y con carácter secreto y, sobre todo, volverá. Bienvenido a casa.

Christiane Reiter

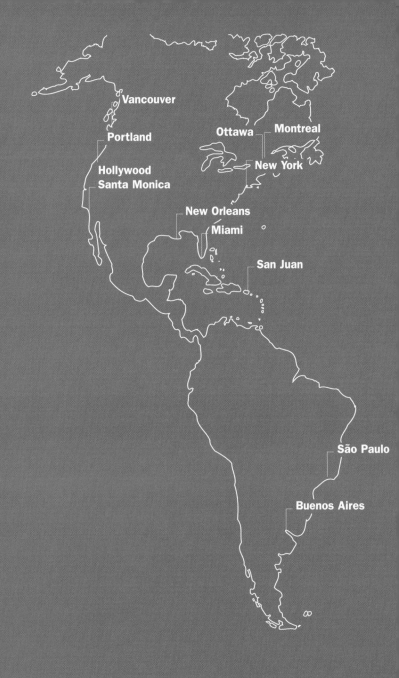

AMERICAS

16 Hotel St Paul Montreal, Canada

HOTEL ST PAUL

Website	www.hotelstpaul.com
Opening date	2000
Address	355 rue McGill
	Montreal, Quebec H2Y 2E8
	Canada
Phone	+1 514 380 2220
Fax	+1 514 380 2200
Rooms	120 rooms including 24 Suiten
Description	business center, 2 meeting rooms for up to 90 people, restaurant, 2 bars, fitness room, library situated in Old Montreal
Architecture/Design	Alexander C. Hutchison (original building) Carlos Aparicio restored by LeMoyne Lapointe Magne Architects Ana Borrallo

HÔTEL LE GERMAIN

Website	www.hotelgermain.com
Opening date	1999
Address	2050 rue Mansfield
	Montreal, Quebec H3A 1Y9
	Canada
Phone	+1 514 849 2050
Fax	+1 514 849 1437
Rooms	101 rooms including 2 executive suites
Description	2 meeting rooms for up to 20 people
Architecture/Design	Lemay Michaud Architecture Design
	Alfred Dallaire
	J. F. Lenoir, Michel Tremblay, Brian Merret,
	Nicolas Koenig, Alain Richer

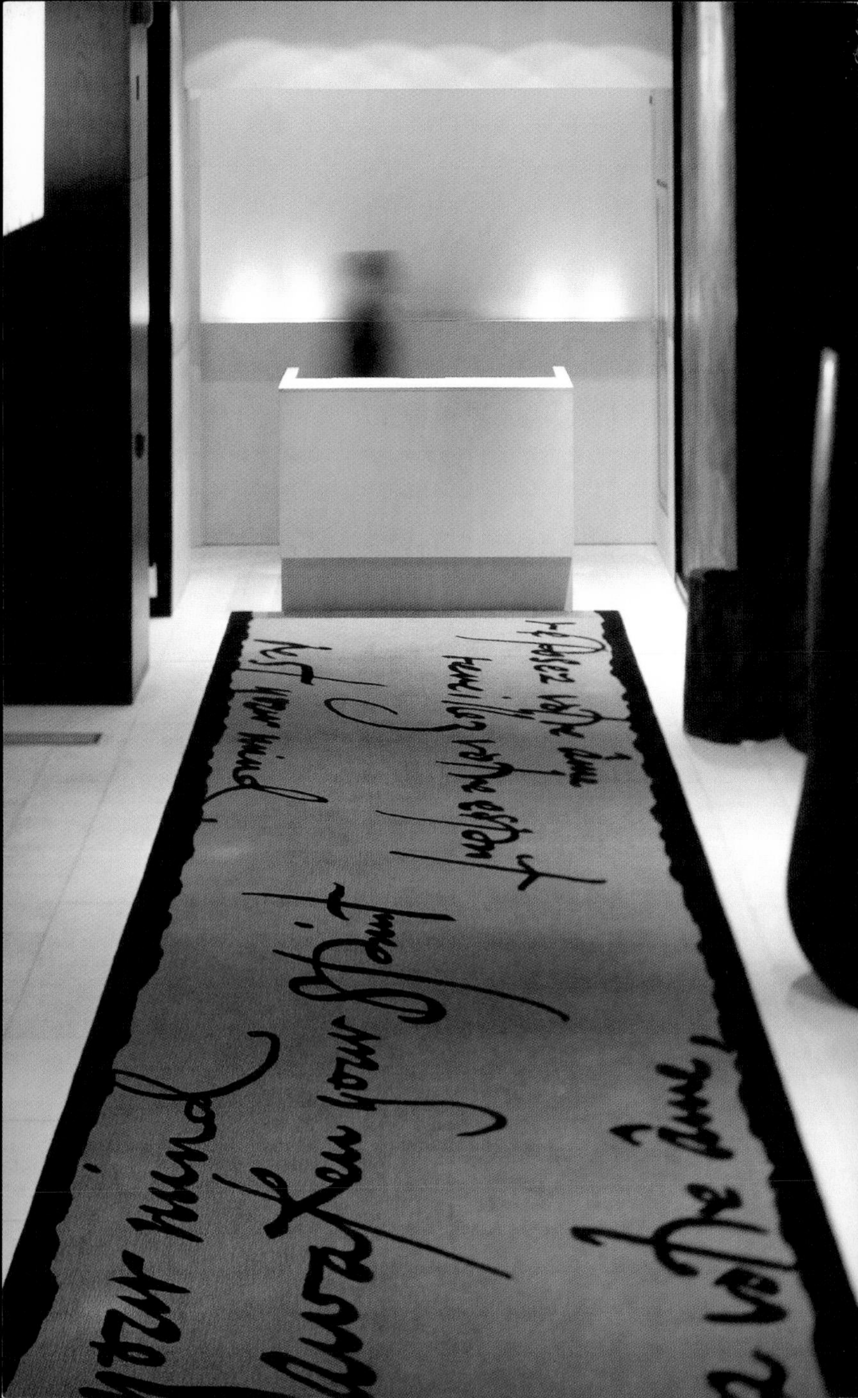

ARC THE.HOTEL

Website	www.arcthehotel.com
Opening date	2000
Address	140 Slater Street
	Ottawa, Ontario K1P 5H6
	Canada
Phone	+1 613 238 2888
Fax	+1 613 235 8421
Rooms	112 rooms including 2 executive suites, 6 junior suites and 7 with roman tub
Description	ARC lounge with restaurant and bar, meeting room, gym
	in the heart of business district of Ottawa
Architecture/Design	Yabu Pushelberg

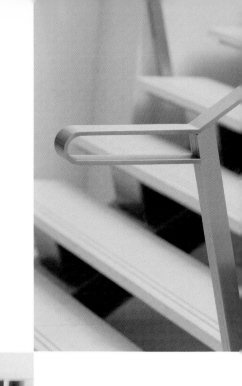

OPUS HOTEL

Website	www.opushotel.com
Opening date	2002
Address	322 Davie Street
	Vancouver, British Columbia U6B 5Z6
	Canada
Phone	+1 604 642 6787
Fax	+1 604 642 6780
Rooms	97 rooms and suites
Description	restaurant Elixier, Opus Bar, Italian coffee bar
	situated in the heart of the historic and
	fashionable Yaletown District, 30 minutes from the
	Vancouver Airport and steps away from
	Vancouver's most spots
Architecture/Design	Paul Merrick Architects
	Architectura Planning Architecture Interiors Inc.
	Hancock, Bruckner, Eng & Wright

Hotel Lucia

Website	www.hotellucia.com
Opening date	2002
Address	400 SW Broadway
	Portland, Oregon 97205
	USA
Phone	+1 503 225 1717
Fax	+1 503 225 1919
Rooms	128 rooms
Description	Typhoon restaurant with Thai haute-cuisine,
	fitness center, business services
	located in the heart of downtown Portland
Architecture/Design	Ankrom Moisan of Portland

Chateau Marmont

Website	www.chateaumarmont.com
Opening date	built 1929, renovated 1990
Address	8221 Sunset Boulevard
	West Hollywood, California 90046
	USA
Phone	+1 323 656 1010
Fax	+1 323 655 5311
Rooms	63 rooms including bungalows, penthouses
	and cottages
Description	restaurant and bar Marmont, outdoor pool, fitness
	room, private garden
	close to the hot spots in Hollywood
Architecture/Design	Shawn Hausman
	Fernando Santangelo
	Craig Ellwood

Sunset Marquis Hotel and Villas

Website	www.sunsetmarquishotel.com
Opening date	reopened 2001
Address	1200 Alta Loma Road
	West Hollywood, California 90069
	USA
Phone	+1 310 657 1333
Fax	+1 310 657 1330
Rooms	108 suites, 12 multi-room villas
Description	restaurant The Room, Whiskey Bar, koi pond,
	jacuzzi, sauna, exercise room, business services,
	in-house recording studio
	close to Sunset Boulevard
Architecture/Design	Oliva Villaluz
	Barry Salehian

THE AMBROSE HOTEL

Website	www.ambrosehotel.com
Opening date	2002
Address	1255 20th Street
	Santa Monica, California 90404
	USA
Phone	+1 310 315 1555
Fax	+1 310 315 1556
Rooms	77 rooms
Description	lounge with fireplace and internet terminal,
	healthful breakfast, fitness facility
	located in the heart of Santa Monica
Architecture/Design	Hank Warner
	Deidre Wallace

Loft 523

Website	www.loft523.com
Opening date	2002
Address	523 Gravier Street
	New Orleans, Louisiana 70130
	USA
Phone	+1 504 200 6523
Fax	+1 504 200 6522
Rooms	18 rooms (15 lofts, 3 penthouses)
Description	bar with private grotto room
	located in New Orleans' business district,
	two blocks away from the historic French Quarter
Architecture/Design	Chrestia, Staub & Pierce

THE SHORE CLUB

Website	www.shoreclub.com
Opening date	2003
Address	1901 Collins Avenue
	South Beach, Miami, Florida 33139
	USA
Phone	+1 305 695 3100
Fax	+1 305 695 3277
Rooms	400 rooms including 70 suites and 5 villas
Description	two world-class restaurants, rooftop spa, two
	swimming pools, direct beach access
	20 minutes from Miami International Airport
Architecture/Design	David Chipperfield
	Miranda Brooks

TIDES

Website	www.islandoutpost.com/tides
Opening date	built 1936, reopened 1997
Address	1220 Ocean Drive
	Miami Beach, Florida 33139
	USA
Phone	+1 305 604 5070
Fax	+1 305 604 5180
Rooms	45 suites including 3 penthouse suites
Description	restaurant, terrace restaurant, lounge bar,
	swimming pool
	located on the beachfront in the heart of the
	Art Deco District
Architecture/Design	Stuart & Ilija Moscrop
	L. Murray Dixon (original building)

THE BRYANT PARK

Website	www.bryantparkhotel.com
Opening date	built 1924, opening 2001
Address	40 W 40th Street
	New York, New York 10018
	USA
Phone	+1 212 869 0100
Fax	+1 212 869 4446
Rooms	149 rooms including 20 suites, 11 with terraces, 2 penthouses
Description	3 star restaurant Ilo, lobby bar and cellar bar, conference room for up to 70 people, screening room, fitness center, spa
	located in Midtown across Bryant Park
Architecture/Design	David Chipperfield
	Raymond Hood, André Fouilhoux (original building)

CHAMBERS A HOTEL

Website	www.chambersnyc.com
Opening date	2000
Address	15 W 56th Street
	New York, New York 10019
	USA
Phone	+1 212 974 5656
Fax	+1 212 974 5657
Rooms	77 rooms including 5 suites
Description	restaurant Town, lobby bar and library, large
	collection of modern art
	situated just off Fifth Avenue
Architecture/Design	David Rockwell

SIXTY THOMPSON

Website	www.60thompson.com
Opening date	2000
Address	60 Thompson Street
	New York, New York 10012
	USA
Phone	+1 212 204 6465
Fax	+1 212 431 0200
Rooms	100 rooms including suites, duplex penthouse
	overlooking Manhattan
Description	restaurant in year-round enclosed terrace,
	THOM restaurant, lounge bar, street side café
	located in the heart of SoHo
Architecture/Design	Steven B. Jacobs
	Thomas O'Brien (Aero Studios)

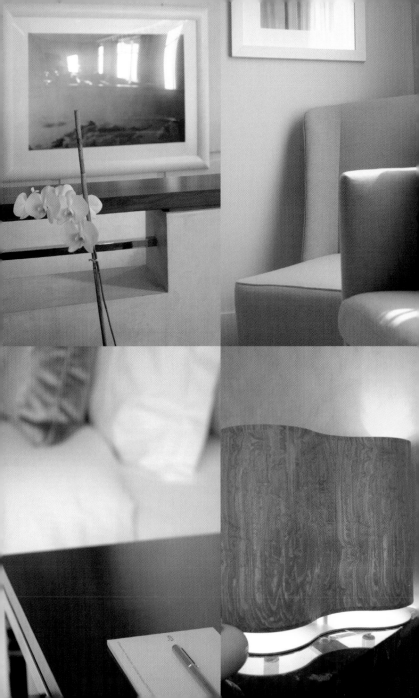

THE TIME

Website	www.thetimeny.com
Opening date	1999
Address	224 W 49th Street
	New York, New York 10019
	USA
Phone	+1 212 980 9060
Fax	+1 212 245 2305
Rooms	164 guest rooms, 29 suites including
	a triplex penthouse
Description	restaurant Coco Pazzo Teatro, The Time Lounge,
	meeting space for up to 35 people
	located in the theater district
Architecture/Design	Adam D. Tihany

W TIMES SQUARE

Website	www.whotels.com
Opening date	2002
Address	1567 Broadway / 47th St
	New York, New York 10036
	USA
Phone	+1 212 930 7400
Fax	+1 212 930 7500
Rooms	509 rooms including 43 suites
Description	Blue Fin restaurant, The Whiskey nightclub,
	6 meeting studios for 10 to 100 people
	located on vibrant Times Square
Architecture/Design	Yabu Pushelberg

The Water Club

Website	www.waterclubsanjuan.com
Opening date	2001
Address	2 Tartak Street
	Isla Verde, San Juan
	Carolina, Puerto Rico 00979
Phone	+1 787 728 3666
Fax	+1 787 728 3610
Rooms	84 ocean front guest rooms and suites
Description	conference facilities, restaurant, bar,
	spa facilities, sundeck and pool on roof top
	located on the beach in Isla Verde, 10 minutes
	from the airport
Architecture/Design	Annie Salgas
	Pedro Rosario
	Designworks Inc

DESIGN SUITES

Website	www.designsuites.com
Opening date	1999
Address	Marcelo T. de Alvear 1683
	Buenos Aires, 1060
	Argentina
Phone	+54 11 4814 8700
Fax	+54 11 4814 8700
Rooms	40 guest rooms
Description	meeting room for up to 60 people, bar, cafeteria, swimming pool, fitness center
	located in Barrio Norte, in the center of Buenos Aires, 1 block away from Santa Fe and Callao
Architecture/Design	Ernesto Goransky

Hotel Unique

Website	www.hotelunique.com.br
Opening date	2003
Address	Av Brigadeiro Luís Antônio, 4700
	Jd. Paulista, São Paulo, CEP 01402-002
	Brazil
Phone	+55 11 3055 4710
Fax	+55 11 3889 8100
Rooms	95 apartments
Description	conference facilities up to 1.200 people, Skye gastronomy on the penthouse level, lobby with Wall Bar and cyber café, library, health club, rooftop swimming pool
Architecture/Design	Ruy Ohtake
	Joao Armentano
	Gilberto Elkis (landscape design)

EUROPE

HOTEL BIRGER JARL

Website	www.birgerjarl.se
Opening date	1999
Address	Tulegatan 8
	10432 Stockholm
	Sweden
Phone	+46 8 674 1800
Fax	+46 8 673 7366
Rooms	240 rooms including 12 signature rooms
	and suites
Description	5 conference rooms up to 150 people, 5 group
	rooms and a banqueting hall
Architecture/Design	Franz Hardinger

NORDIC LIGHT HOTEL

Website	www.nordichotels.se
Opening date	2000
Address	Vasaplan, Box 884
	10137 Stockholm
	Sweden
Phone	+46 8 5056 3000
Fax	+46 8 5056 3060
Rooms	175 rooms ranging from XS to XL
Description	L-Dine restaurant, L-Bar and famous Ice Bar in
	sister property Nordic Sea Hotel on the other side
	of the street, conference and business center
	relaxation zone, sauna, jacuzzi
	located in the center of Stockholm
Architecture/Design	Lars Pihl
	Jan Söder
	Rolf Löfvenberg

RADISSON SAS ROYAL HOTEL

Website	www.radissonsas.com
Opening date	opening 1960, reopening 2001
Address	Hammerichsgade 1
	Copenhagen, DK-1611
	Denmark
Phone	+45 33 42 60 00
Fax	+45 33 42 61 00
Rooms	260 rooms including 3 suites
Description	gourmet restaurant Alberto K in the 20th floor
	overlooking the city, Cafe Royal, Orchid Bar,
	large business facilities, spa
	in the city center across from Tivoli Garden
Architecture/Design	Arne Jacobsen
	Yasmine Mahmoudieh

THE GLASSHOUSE

Website	www.etontownhouse.com
Opening date	2003
Address	2 Greenside Place
	Edinburgh EH1 3AA
	United Kingdom
Phone	+44 131 525 8200
Fax	+44 131 525 8205
Rooms	65 rooms including 13 studio suites and 5 suites
Description	rooftop garden, drawing room with Honesty Bar, 3 meeting rooms for up to 70 people
	located at the foot of Calton Hill in the heart of the city, next door to the Edinburgh Playhouse and just a few steps from Princes Street and Edinburgh Castle
Architecture/Design	Cobban Lironi Weddell & Thomas

174 The Glasshouse   Edinburgh, United Kingdom

CHARLOTTE STREET HOTEL

Website	www.charlottestreethotel.com
Opening date	2000
Address	15–17 Charlotte Street
	London W1T 1RJ
	United Kingdom
Phone	+44 20 7806 2000
Fax	+44 20 7806 2002
Rooms	52 rooms and suites
Description	Oscar bar and restaurant, 2 meeting rooms, video conferencing, screening & drawing room, library with fireplace, gym
	located in the media and entertainment area near Soho square
Architecture/Design	Kit Kemp

SHERLOCK HOLMES HOTEL

Website	www.sherlockholmeshotel.com
Opening date	2001
Address	108 Baker Street
	London W1U 6LJ
	United Kingdom
Phone	+44 20 7958 5222
Fax	+44 20 7958 5223
Rooms	119 rooms including 17 executive studios
	and 3 loft suites
Description	Sherlock's Bar and Grill, 7 meeting rooms for up
	to 50 people, treatment room, gym
	walking distance to Madame Tussauds, the
	London Planetarium, Hyde Park, Oxford Street,
	Bond Street and Regents Street
Architecture/Design	EAA international

Sherlock Holmes Hotel   London, United Kingdom   **189**

THE LOWRY HOTEL

Website	www.thelowryhotel.com
Opening date	2001
Address	50 Dearmans Place
	Chapel Wharf
	Manchester M3 5LH
	United Kingdom
Phone	+44 161 827 4000
Fax	+44 161 827 4001
Rooms	165 rooms including 6 suites, the Charles Forte suite and 9 rooms with facilities for disabled
Description	Pierre White restaurant, meeting facilities for up to 400 people, River Room Marco, holistic health and fitness center
	situated in the heart of the city
Architecture/Design	Consarc Design Architects
	Jarvis Construction

HOTEL BRANDENBURGER HOF

Website	www.brandenburgerhof.com
Opening date	1991
Address	Eislebener Straße 14
	10789 Berlin
	Germany
Phone	+49 30 21405 0
Fax	+49 30 21405 100
Rooms	82 rooms including 4 suites
Description	gourmet restaurant Quadriga, piano bar,
	restaurant Wintergarten, library, wine-cellar,
	3 salons for 10 to 40 people, wintergarden for
	90 people, presentations possible for up to
	350 people, beauty and massage suite
	in walking distance to Kurfürstendamm
Architecture/Design	Peter Sauter
	Kenji Tsuchiya

200 Hotel Brandenburger Hof   Berlin, Germany

GRAND HYATT BERLIN

Website	www.berlin.grand.hyatt.de
Opening date	1998
Address	Marlene-Dietrich-Platz 2
	10785 Berlin
	Germany
Phone	+49 30 2553 1234
Fax	+49 30 2553 1235
Rooms	326 rooms, 16 suites including
	2 presidential suites
Description	3 restaurants, 7 meeting room, ballroom for up to
	850 people, Club Olympus Spa & Fitness in upper
	floor
	directly at Potsdamer Platz
Architecture/Design	José Rafael Moneo
	Hannes Wettstein

MADISON POTSDAMER PLATZ

Website	www.madison-berlin.de
Opening date	1999
Address	Potsdamer Straße 3
	10785 Berlin
	Germany
Phone	+49 30 590 05 0000
Fax	+49 30 590 05 00
Rooms	167 suites
Description	restaurant Facil, qui Lounge, fitness lounge, spa, shopping service for daily demand, 3 meeting rooms for up to 20 people
Architecture/Design	Lauber und Wöhr
	Flum Design

DORINT AM ALTEN WALL

Website	www.dorint.de/hamburg-city
Opening date	2000
Address	Alter Wall 40
	20457 Hamburg
	Germany
Phone	+49 40 36 95 00
Fax	+49 40 36 95 01 000
Rooms	216 guest rooms, 17 suites and 8 studio rooms
Description	2 restaurants, Seven Heads Bar, cigar lounge
	smokers club, indoor swimming pool, sauna,
	solarium, fitness room, 19 conference rooms for
	up to 380 people
	located in the city center
Architecture/Design	Harald Klein
	Bert Haller

CORTIINA HOTEL

Website	www.cortiina.com
Opening date	2001
Address	Ledererstraße 8
	80331 München
	Germany
Phone	+49 89 242 2490
Fax	+49 89 242 249100
Rooms	33 rooms
Description	located in the historical heart of Munich,
	just some minutes away from opera, theater,
	Maximilianstraße and Viktualienmarkt
Architecture/Design	Albert Weinzierl

RAMADA PLAZA BASEL

Website	www.ramada-treff.ch
Opening date	2003
Address	Messeplatz 12
	4058 Basel
	Switzerland
Phone	+41 61 560 4000
Fax	+41 61 560 5555
Rooms	230 rooms
Description	restaurant Filou, Timeless Bar, lobby bar,
	conference area, wellness area with sauna and
	steam bath
	located at the Messeplatz exhibition center
Architecture/Design	Meinrad Morger
	Helmut Vorreiter

Ramada Plaza Basel   Basel, Switzerland   **239**

Hôtel Angleterre & Résidence

Website	www.angleterre-residence.ch
Opening date	reopened 2002
Address	Place du Port 11
	1006 Lausanne
	Switzerland
Phone	+41 21 613 3434
Fax	+41 21 613 3435
Rooms	74 rooms in 4 buildings
Description	restaurant L'Accademia, Le Bistro, La Voûte,
	4 meeting rooms for up to 72 people
	bordering Lake Geneva, 5 minutes walking
	distance to the city of Lausanne
Architecture/Design	Danilo Mondada
	Christopher Amsler
	Dominique Couture
	Francois Bertin

246 Hôtel Angleterre & Résidence   Lausanne, Switzerland

Hotel Josef

Website	www.hoteljosef.com
Opening date	2002
Address	Rybná 20
	110 00 Prague 1
	Czech Republic
Phone	+420 2 2170 0111
Fax	+420 2 2170 0999
Rooms	110 rooms
Description	restaurant, bar 3 conference rooms for up to
	90 people
	located in the city centre of Prague, 5 minutes
	walking distance from the Old Town Square
Architecture/Design	Eva Jiricna

LE DOKHAN'S

Website	www.sofitel-paris.com
Opening date	1999
Address	117, rue Lauriston
	75116 Paris
	France
Phone	+33 1 5365 6699
Fax	+33 1 5365 6688
Rooms	45 rooms including 4 suites
Description	restaurant, bar
	located at Trocadéro, 10 minutes walk
	to Eiffel Tower
Architecture/Design	Frédéric Méchiche

Hôtel de la Trémoille

Website	www.hotel-tremoille.com
Opening date	reopening 2002
Address	14, rue de la Trémoille
	75008 Paris
	France
Phone	+33 1 5652 1400
Fax	+33 1 4070 0108
Rooms	93 rooms, including 23 standard rooms,
	43 superior rooms, 14 deluxe rooms, 8 junior
	suites and 5 deluxe suites
Description	Senso restaurant and bar, 2 meeting rooms for
	up to 30 people, cardio-training center, sauna,
	hydro-jet shower, 2 private care rooms
	in the heart of Paris' Golden Triangle in the 8th
	arrondissement at the corner of rue de la
	Trémoille and Boccador
Architecture/Design	Richard Martinet

J.K. PLACE

Website	www.jkplace.com
Opening date	2003
Address	Piazza Santa Maria Novella, 7
	50123 Florence
	Italy
Phone	+39 055 264 5181
Fax	+39 055 265 8387
Rooms	20 rooms and suites
Description	in the heart of Florence at Piazza Santa Maria Novella, just a few steps from the Renaissance church Santa Maria Novella
Architecture/Design	Michele Bonan

ENTERPRISE HOTEL

Website	www.enterprisehotel.com
Opening date	2002
Address	Corso Sempione, 91
	20154 Milan
	Italy
Phone	+39 02 3181 81
Fax	+39 02 3181 8811
Rooms	109 rooms including 5 junior suites, 2 suites, 11 apartments
Description	Sophia's Restaurant, 2 bars, wine cellar, 8 meeting rooms
	located in the commercial quarter, close to the Fair
Architecture/Design	Sofia Gioia Vedani
	Christina Di Carlo
	Christopher Redfern

ALEPH

Website	www.aleph.boscolohotels.com
Opening date	2003
Address	Via di San Basilio, 15
	00187 Rome
	Italy
Phone	+39 06 422 901
Fax	+39 06 422 90000
Rooms	99 rooms including 2 suites with jacuzzi
Description	restaurant, bar & wine lounge, library,
	rooftop terrace café, spa area with turkish bath,
	sauna, pools
	located in the heart of Rome, 5 minutes
	from station Termini
Architecture/Design	Adam D. Tihany

Hotel Arts Barcelona

Website	www.ritzcarlton.com/hotels/barcelona
Opening date	1992
Address	Carrer de la Marina, 19–21
	08005 Barcelona
	Spain
Phone	+34 93 221 1000
Fax	+34 93 221 1070
Rooms	482 rooms including 44 executive suites, 32 deluxe rooms and 12 executive suites on The Club, 27 duplex luxury apartments
Description	restaurants and bars with outdoor terraces, garden and outdoor swimming pool, extensive meeting and function rooms
Architecture/Design	Skidmore, Owings & Merrill LLP
	Robert Brufau y Asociados
	Frank Gehry (metallic fish sculpture)

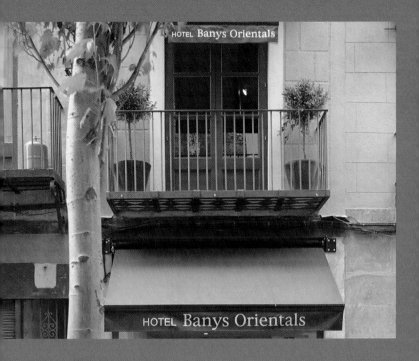

HOTEL BANYS ORIENTALS

Website	www.hotelbanysorientals.com
Opening date	2000
Address	C. Argenteria, 37
	08003 Barcelona
	Spain
Phone	+34 93 268 8460
Rooms	+34 93 268 8461
Description	43 rooms
	restaurant Senyor Parellada with authentical
	Catalan kitchen
	in the Born district near the Cathedral and the
	Gothic district, within 10 minutes to the ocean
Architecture/Design	Lazaro Rosa

GRAN HOTEL DOMINE

Website	www.granhoteldominebilbao.com
Opening date	2002
Address	Alameda de Mazarredo, 61
	48009 Bilbao
	Spain
Phone	+34 944 253 300
Fax	+34 944 253 301
Rooms	145 rooms including 14 suites
Description	cafeteria, cocktail lounge, restaurant, reading corner
	facing the Guggenheim Museum
Architecture/Design	Inaki Aurrecoetxea
	Javier Mariscal
	Fernando Salas

Gran Hotel Domine   Bilbao, Spain   **313**

316 Gran Hotel Domine Bilbao, Spain

Solar Do Castelo

Website	www.heritage.pt/en/solardocastelo.htm
Opening date	2001
Address	Rua das Cozinhas, 2 (ao Castelo)
	1100–181 Lisbon
	Portugal
Phone	+351 218 870 909
Fax	+351 218 870 907
Rooms	14 rooms
Description	breakfast buffet in the garden, library, honour bar
	located in the former kitchen mansion
	of Castelo S. Jorge
Architecture/Design	Vasco Massapina
	Graca Viterbo

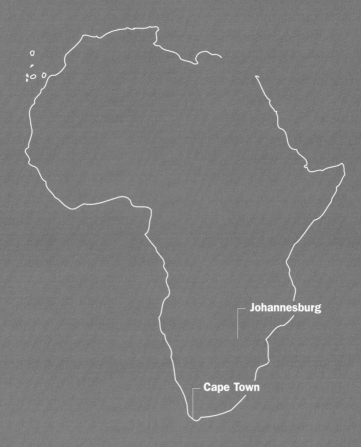

Johannesburg

Cape Town

AFRICA

TEN BOMPAS

Website	www.tenbompas.com
Opening date	1996
Address	10 Bompas Road
	Dunkeld West, Sandton 2146
	Gauteng, Johannesburg
	South Africa
Phone	+27 11 325 2442
Fax	+27 11 341 0281
Rooms	10 suites
Description	Sides restaurant, steam baths, pool, health club membership, nearby golf course, 2 meeting rooms for up to 20 people
Architecture/Design	Luc Zeghers & Associates

334 Ten Bompas Johannesburg, South Africa

Saxon

Website	www.thesaxon.com
Opening date	reopening 2000
Address	36 Saxon Road, Sandhurst
	Johannesburg
	South Africa
Phone	+27 11 292 6000
Fax	+27 11 292 6001
Rooms	26 suites including 20 Egoli suites, 4 presidential suites and 2 platinum suites
Description	restaurant, wine-cellar with private dining room, 3 meeting rooms for up to 40 people, outdoor pool with under water music, fitness studio, park
Architecture/Design	Neil Powell
	Clive Shepard and Louw Ridley
	Stephen Falcke Interiors
	Patrick Watson (landscape design)

342 Saxon   Johannesburg, South Africa

346 Saxon   Johannesburg, South Africa

KENSINGTON PLACE

Website	www.kensingtonplace.co.za
Opening date	1996
Address	38 Kensington Crescent, Higgovale
	Cape Town, 8001
	South Africa
Phone	+27 21 424 4744
Fax	+27 21 424 1810
Rooms	8 rooms with private terraces
Description	contemporary interiors with eclectic African
	touches throughout
	located on the slopes of Table Mountain
Architecture/Design	Anton De Kok
	Kobus De Vos

ASIA &
AUSTRALIA

THE PARK BANGALORE

Website	www.theparkhotels.com
Opening date	2001
Address	14/7 Mahatma Gandhi Road
	Bangalore – 560 001
	India
Phone	+91 80 559 4666
Fax	+91 80 559 4667
Rooms	109 rooms including suites
Description	Monsoon + I.t-ALIA restaurant, i-BAR lounge bar,
	banquete hall for up to 150 people, screening
	room for up to 25 people
	6 kilometers from the airport
Architecture/Design	Conran & Partners

THE STRAND

Website	www.ghmhotels.com/thestrand
Opening date	built 1901, reopened 1993
Address	92 Strand Road
	Yangon
	Myanmar
Phone	+95 1 243 377
Fax	+95 1 289 880
Rooms	32 deluxe and superior suites, "The Strand Suite"
Description	restaurant, bar, café, business center
Architecture/Design	David Wordsworth
	Leigh & Orange Co. Ltd. Hongkong

368 The Strand   Yangon, Myanmar

THE FULLERTON

Website	www.fullertonhotel.com
Opening date	built 1928, hotel opening 2001
Address	1 Fullerton Square
	Singapore 049178
	Singapore
Phone	+65 6733 8388
Fax	+65 6735 8388
Rooms	400 rooms including 35 suites and the Straits Club
Description	restaurants and bars, 12 meeting rooms, asian spa
	located in the heart of the central business district, fronting the Marina Bay
Architecture/Design	Keys & Dowdeswell
	Architects 61 Pte Ltd
	Hirscher Bedner Associates Pte Ltd

378 The Fullerton   Singapore, Singapore

HOTEL LINDRUM

Website	www.hotellindrum.com.au
Opening date	1999
Address	26 Flinders Street
	Melbourne, Victoria 3000
	Australia
Phone	+61 3 9668 1111
Fax	+61 3 9668 1199
Rooms	59 rooms and suites
Description	restaurant, bar, dining room, conference room, library, billard room, lounge with open fireplace located in the center of Melbourne
Architecture/Design	Swaney Draper Architects
	Terry Fripp
	Neil Bradford

ESTABLISHMENT

Website	www.luxehotels.com/hotels/93.html
Opening date	2000
Address	5 Bridge Lane
	Sydney, New South Wales 2000
	Australia
Phone	+61 2 9240 3000
Fax	+61 2 9240 3101
Rooms	33 deluxe rooms and 2 penthouse suites
Description	Establishment Bar, Garden Bar, Tank Stream Bar,
	sushi bar, Est. Restaurant, ballroom for up
	to 400 people, 3 conference rooms
	located in Sydney's business district in walking
	distance to the most attractions
Architecture/Design	Crone & Associates
	SJB
	Andrew Parr

396 Establishment Sydney, Australia

Photo Credits

Other Designpocket titles by teNeues:

Asian Interior Design 3-8238-4527-6
Bathroom Design 3-8238-4523-3
Berlin Apartments 3-8238-5596-4
Cafés & Restaurants 3-8238-5478-X
Cool Hotels 3-8238-5556-5
Country Hotels 3-8238-5574-3
Exhibition Design 3-8238-5548-4
Furniture Design 3-8238-5575-1
Garden Design 3-8238-4524-1
Italian Interior Design 3-8238-5495-X
Kitchen Design 3-8238-4522-5
London Apartments 3-8238-5558-1
Los Angeles Houses 3-8238-5594-8
Miami Houses 3-8238-4545-4
New York Apartments 3-8238-5557-3
Office Design 3-8238-5578-6
Paris Apartments 3-8238-5571-9
Pool Design 3-8238-4531-4
Product Design 3-8238-5597-2
San Francisco Houses 3-8238-4526-8
Showrooms 3-8238-5496-8
Ski Hotels 3-8238-4543-8
Spa & Wellness Hotels 3-8238-5595-6
Staircases 3-8238-5572-7
Sydney Houses 3-8238-4525-X
Tokyo Houses 3-8238-5573-5
Tropical Houses 3-8238-4544-6

Each volume:

12.5 x 18.5 cm
400 pages
c. 400 color illustrations